Making Tiffany Lamps

Making Tiffany Lamps

How to Create Museum-Quality Authentic Reproductions

Hugh V. Archer

photographs by Alan Wycheck

STACKPOLE
BOOKS

Copyright 2009 by Stackpole Books

Published by
STACKPOLE BOOKS
5067 Ritter Road
Mechanicsburg, PA 17055
www.stackpolebooks.com

Printed in China

10 9 8 7 6 5 4 3 2 1

First edition

Cover design by Wendy A. Reynolds

All lampshades shown in this book were made by the author.

Library of Congress Cataloging-in-Publication Data

Archer, Hugh.
    Making Tiffany lamps : how to create museum-quality
authentic reproductions / Hugh Archer ; photographs by Alan
Wycheck.
        p.   cm.
    Includes bibliographical references.
    ISBN-13: 978-0-8117-3595-7
    ISBN-10: 0-8117-3595-8
    1. Glass craft—Patterns. 2. Glass painting and staining—
Patterns. 3. Glass lampshades. I. Title.
TT298.A78 2009
748.5028—dc22
                                                            2009002026

Contents

The Tiffany Legacy

Louis Comfort Tiffany (1848–1933), American artist and son of Charles Lewis Tiffany, founder of the jewelry firm Tiffany & Co., used art glass and artificial lighting to express his lasting love of nature and left us with perhaps the most significant contribution to the artistic movement known as Art Nouveau. Louis Comfort Tiffany's initial venture into the world of leaded glass was focused solely on windows. Most of these depicted Art Nouveau and/or religious themes and were considered individual works of art. Commercial production of his art-glass lamps, all designed to follow some geometric or floral form, was largely inspired by Thomas Edison's invention of the incandescent light bulb. The lamps, most of which were produced in the 1900s through the 1920s, originally sold for $100 to $200. Unlike the windows, the lamps were not at the time considered artistic accomplishments, perhaps because they mostly featured repeated individual designs (even today, lamps that were produced as commissioned pieces and feature one-of-a-kind designs have the highest value).

After Tiffany's death, his lamps lost commercial popularity, and many were discarded as trash. Today, the lamps that originally sold for $100 can be worth $30,000 to $300,000, and unique single-production lamps have sold at auction for more than a million dollars.

In the late 1960s and early 1970s, an awareness of the beauty and value of Tiffany lamps steadily grew as the originals began to be considered antiques. Because of high asking prices and this renewed public interest, a few commercial art-glass studios began producing high-quality reproductions of original lamps for resale. These reproductions were, in some cases, better constructed than the originals, but they sold for only a fraction of the value of an authentic lamp. The creation of these reproductions was severely hampered by the limited access to original shades in order to accurately copy the pattern.

Eventually, entrepreneurs realized that producing the lamps overseas would reduce labor costs and asking prices for so-called Tiffany lamps while increasing volumes and, subsequently, profits. Today, the Tiffany reproduction market has largely been replaced by offshore-produced "Tiffany inspired" lamps and inexpensive bases, which are usually sold at interior lighting stores. At the same time, however, a growing number of individual lamp artists began making authentic reproduction lamps by hand, and the best of these have steadily increased in value.

Authentic Reproductions

As the name implies, a true reproduction Tiffany lamp pattern has to be an exact copy or rubbing from an original lamp. Rubbings are made by covering an original shade with paper and rubbing over the lamp's raised lead lines with a pencil, which accurately transfers the pattern to the paper. Access to accomplish this is usually

Workshop Safety

Health and safety in the art-glass workshop is very important, as a number of potentially harmful chemicals and chemical compounds are used in lamp construction. Care must be taken at all times to avoid inhaling fumes or ingesting inorganic particulate materials from fluxes, cleaning compounds, patinas, and the waste materials from solder and lead. First and foremost, the workshop should have a good system of ventilation that offers 2 or 3 full air changes per hour.

Other cardinal health and safety rules are as follows:

- Never take food or drink into the workshop.
- Always wear protective gear—apron, gloves, and safety goggles—and, when finished working, wash your hands thoroughly.
- Before mixing or using any chemicals, read and follow the instructions and note the warnings given on the labels.
- The workshop should be well lit as well as adequately ventilated, especially when soldering or applying chemicals.
- Keep the workshop clean and properly dispose of all used chemicals, waste compounds, and lead chips.

available only to artists who have been commissioned to repair an original shade or who have an original shade in their possession.

There are a number of companies that make Tiffany-inspired lamp molds for the general public. The largest is the H. L. Worden Lamp Crafting System. Worden offers a variety of lamp patterns, most of which are interpretations of original Tiffany designs, and some are original Art Nouveau designs. Worden molds are made of styrofoam, and the pattern comes in segments that are pinned to the mold. Worden molds and patterns are inexpensive and easy to use.

The Whittemore-Durgin Glass Company offers a limited number of full-form fiberglass molds and patterns that are also interpretations of original Tiffany designs. These molds are more expensive than Worden's but are

also more durable. Conti Studios also offers a number of full-form fiberglass lamp molds and panel lamp designs featuring Art Nouveau patterns designed by Carol Conti.

The Tiffany lamp patterns and molds that are of the greatest interest to reproduction lamp artists are those in the Odyssey Lamp System. Odyssey offers full-form molds and patterns for Tiffany shades ranging from 10 inches to 28 inches in diameter. All Odyssey patterns are based on rubbings taken directly from original Tiffany lamps: they are truly authentic reproduction molds and patterns. The company also offers reproduction hardware, including caps and wheels, to complement the molds and patterns. In this book, we demonstrate the construction of a 22-inch Elaborate Peony authentic reproduction shade using a mold and pattern from the Odyssey Lamp System.

1. Preparing the Pattern

This book will describe and illustrate in detail the process of creating an authentic reproduction Tiffany lampshade. It will cover each step in the process—from cutting apart the pattern to applying the final finish—so an aspiring lamp artist will know exactly what needs to be done to create a one-of-a-kind Tiffany shade.

The 22-inch-diameter Elaborate Peony pattern comprises 1,038 individual glass pieces and is one of the larger shades Tiffany made. This peony shade takes a 5-inch brass ring as reinforcement for the aperture and a $^3/_{16}$-inch-diameter brass rod, called a rim, approximately 33 inches long, bent in a circle, to reinforce the bottom of the shade. Three 12-gauge soft copper wires will be used to reinforce the inside of the shade from ring to rim.

Start Small

If this is your first reproduction lamp project, we strongly suggest that you select one of the smaller, simpler lamp molds to start with in order to build a certain level of comfort and expertise. One of the most persistent problems we encounter when teaching classes for first-time lamp reproduction artists is that the students tend to select projects that are too large and/or complicated. They then get discouraged because the project takes so long to complete.

There are a number of smaller projects we would suggest for the beginner. Following is a list of molds (with product numbers) we have found to be good selections for a first project. The selections are all taken from the Odyssey Lamp Systems catalog:

 12-inch Dogwood (T-1417)

 15-inch Spider (T-1424)

 16-inch Woodbine (T-1468)

 16-inch Apple Blossom (T-1455)

 16-inch Poppy (T-1461)

Tiffany reproduction molds made by Odyssey are packaged with an instruction booklet and two patterns, one printed on plain paper and one on mylar.

This 22-inch Elaborate Peony mold is inscribed with the number that corresponds to the original Tiffany pattern. Odyssey molds are based on rubbings of actual Tiffany shades; each glass tile matches exactly the size and shape of the corresponding tile on an original Tiffany lamp.

All Odyssey mold kits come with a sturdy, almost-indestructible fiberglass mold, one paper and one mylar pattern sheet, and an instruction booklet. The booklet suggests that the artist cut apart the mylar sheet into individual pattern pieces, which are then used to trace the outlines on the selected art glass. With today's highly precise copying machines, however, we simply use the mylar sheet to make exact paper copies that are then cut apart using a sharp standard pair of scissors. That way we have a paper pattern piece for every individual glass tile we need to cut—all 1,038 of them.

Cutting Apart the Pattern

After the copies are made, the first step is to cut out each piece in the pattern. Pattern shears, which have three blades and remove the thin strip of paper surrounding the black lines, are not necessary for this step. Because the lines on a lamp pattern already represent the leaded line, a normal pair of sharp scissors is used to cut along each line where it touches the white paper, which effectively eliminates each line.

Using a Jig

If you plan to mount your fiberglass mold on a lamp jig for support during the construction process, you will need to make a plywood platform for the mold. Instructions for doing so, and for mounting the mold to the jig, are included in the Odyssey booklet. This involves cutting a disk out of scrap plywood to be fitted into the base of the mold and held in place with screws, nails, or glue.

While not absolutely necessary, a jig can make the lamp-making process easier. A free-standing lamp jig is typically used for larger lampshades and allows the artist maximum freedom and flexibility when it comes time to solder. Tabletop jigs work well for smaller shades.

Lamp artists can also use foam blocks known as Wedgies, which are especially made for stained glass work. The blocks are heat resistant and not affected by solder flux. These help support a shade in a variety of positions on a work surface to allow good access for soldering, and they don't require you to create the plywood disk. For our shade, we used Wedgies to position the lamp while soldering.

The pattern printed on mylar is intended to be cut apart, but we suggest that photocopies be made for each repeat and that these copies be cut apart. That way the artist will have a pattern piece for every tile on the shade without having to reuse them.

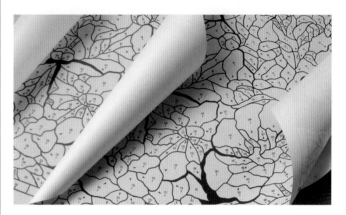

The individual pieces on the pattern are numbered. Arrows on some of the pieces indicate the suggested direction for the grain of the art glass. The blackened areas of the pattern indicate "blank" spaces that will disappear when the tile pieces are affixed to the rounded shade.

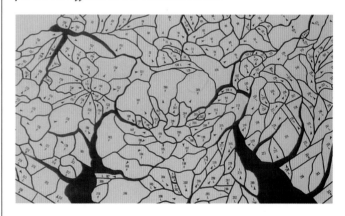

The pattern indicates the total number of pieces in the finished shade, the size of the aperture ring, and the number of repeats required to go all the way around the mold. This 22-inch Elaborate Peony pattern has three repeats, meaning that three pieces of glass must be cut for each individual piece shown on the pattern.

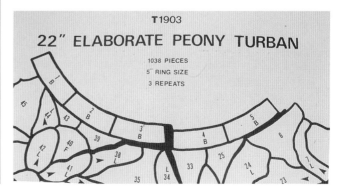

T1903
22" ELABORATE PEONY TURBAN
1038 PIECES
5" RING SIZE
3 REPEATS

The paper pieces are then affixed to the art glass with rubber cement to serve as templates for breaking and grinding. Care should be taken to make exact copies of the mylar pattern: if the glass tiles are even slightly smaller or larger, they will not fit together properly and the finished lamp will not be representative of the original. We always make certain the copies are an exact match by overlaying and comparing the mylar sheet with each copy on a light table.

The Elaborate Peony is a three-repeat pattern, meaning that the outlined section shown on the pattern is reproduced three times to create the entire 22-inch shade. We therefore make four copies of the mylar sheet, cutting apart three of them and leaving one intact for reference. If the pattern has more repeats, you'll need to make a correspondingly larger number of copies.

The cut-apart pieces are then sorted, with the leaves (indicated by an L on the pattern), flower petals (F), stems (S), borders (B), flower centers (C), buds, bracts, and background all kept separately, each in a small baggie. We have found that separating the pieces according to what they represent helps make the process of selecting art glass and affixing the pieces to the glass go much more smoothly.

Note that the pattern pieces are all numbered, and each of our baggies contains three copies of each number. Most of the pattern pieces also have an arrow suggesting in what direction the color and grain of the art glass used for that piece should run. In most cases, all unlettered pieces are for the background.

The pattern pieces are also coded with letters that indicate what each piece is meant to represent. The particular colors and variations used to interpret the peony flowers, buds, stems, and so on are choices made by the artist. There are no right or wrong choices, although some artists prefer to use only flower colors that were available in Tiffany's time, not colors featured on today's hybrid plants.

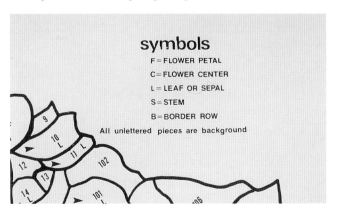

After the pattern copies are cut apart, it's best to keep the pieces of each part of the pattern separated. As portions of art glass are chosen to interpret each piece, the paper pieces are affixed to the glass with rubber cement to serve as a guide for cutting and grinding.

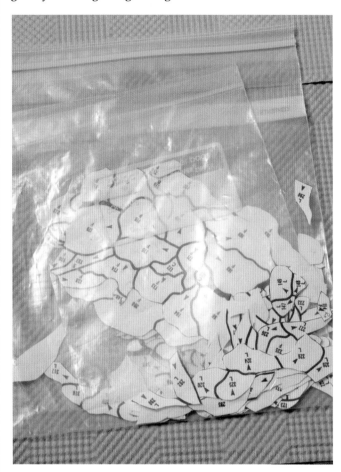

We recommend that beginners assemble a full repeat of their chosen shade on a sheet of clear glass or plastic to make certain that everything will fit together on the mold and that the selected glass and color choices are satisfactory.

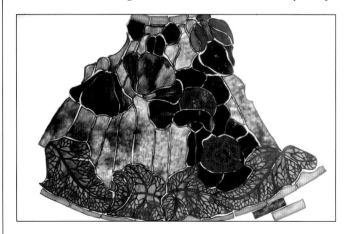

2. Grouting the Mold

Odyssey fiberglass molds come with the pattern lines engraved into the surface, but these lines are not easily visible and need to be highlighted to allow correct placement of the glass tiles. There are two ways to highlight the lines: marking with a pen or grouting. The first method involves using a permanent, black felt-tip pen (such as a Sharpie Fine Point) and carefully going over all the engraved lines. This approach, while effective, is tedious and time consuming, and, if you are not careful, the pen will skip out of the engraved line, marking the mold.

We recommend the second method—using black sandless tile grout—to fill in the engraved lines. This approach is faster and produces better results. While it is possible to make your own grout by mixing pigment, sandless grout, glue, and water, unless you intend to do several molds at once and therefore need a lot of grout, it is more efficient and less costly to simply purchase a 10-ounce container of Odyssey Mold Mud, which is what we are using. To mix up what we need for our 22-inch mold, we place 2 tablespoons of Mold Mud in a plastic container, add a small amount of Elmer's glue and approximately 1 teaspoon of tap water, and stir. Additional water is then added a little at a time to create a thick, soupy consistency.

We then use a damp sponge to smear the mixture over the outer surface of the entire mold, being careful to ensure that the engraved lines are filled with the mud.

When the mold is completely covered with mud, it's left to dry for approximately 15 to 20 minutes. Then we use a slightly dampened, clean piece of sponge or dry paper towels to remove the excess mud from the mold, leaving the engraved lines clearly highlighted.

Lamp molds are incised with lines that serve as a guide for tile placement, but the lines are difficult to see.

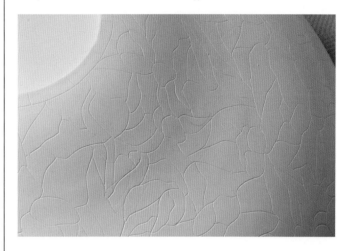

The easiest way to grout a lamp mold is to use a canister of powdered Mold Mud made by Odyssey especially for that purpose.

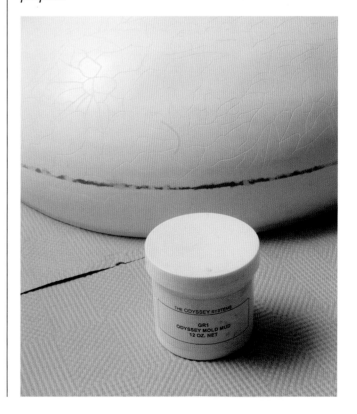

Less than ¹/₂ cup of a grout mixture is needed to cover this 22-inch mold.

Prepare the grout according to the instructions on the canister. Add water a little at a time and stir until the mixture resembles brownie mix. If it's too thin, add more grout; if it's too thick, add more water.

A slightly dampened sponge is used to apply the grout.

Plop some grout onto the shade, then spread it around with the sponge.

Remember that the primary intent is to fill the incised lines with grout. There's no need to be too precise about how much grout you use.

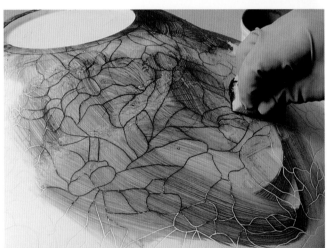

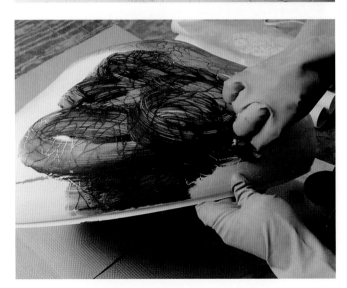

When all the lines are filled with grout, let the mold dry for 15 to 20 minutes.

Use a clean, lightly dampened sponge or heavy-duty paper towel to wipe off the excess grout, being careful not to pull the grout out of the incised lines.

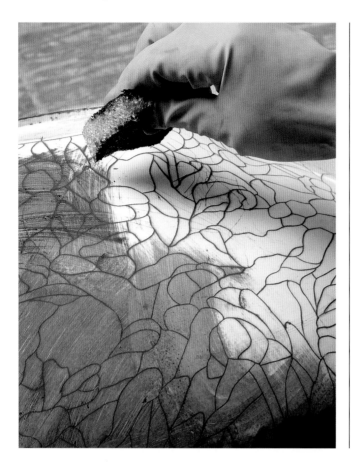

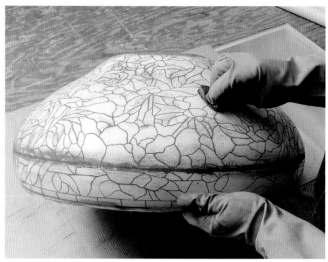

When you're finished, all the lines should be clearly delineated and the surface of the mold should be relatively clean. The grout in the lines will hold up pretty well as the mold is used to create a shade and will probably be ready to use for several other shades without any need for additional grouting.

3. Selecting the Art Glass

areful selection and use of art glass is, without a doubt, the most critically important step in Tiffany lamp reproduction. Even a less-than-perfectly constructed shade can, when lit, take on a beautiful and unique life of its own if it has a distinctive, appealing appearance and color scheme. It would take a separate book to even begin to scratch the surface of educating first-time lamp artists on the types and varieties of art glass and how to best go about selecting and using the glass in Tiffany lamp reproductions. While each artist over time will develop his or her own way of expressing a daffodil flower petal, for example, using color, color flow, and transparency, one of the surest ways to learn the art of glass selection and use is to study as many original Tiffany lamps as possible, either in photographs or in person when possible. Not all Tiffany shades might be masterpieces, but seeing the same design interpreted in different ways offers invaluable lessons for the lamp artist.

One of the largest collections of original Tiffany lamps open to the public is the Neustadt Collection, part of which is on permanent display in the Queens Museum of Art in New York, and part of which makes up a traveling exhibition. Information on the collection is available on the museum's collection website (www.neustadtcollection.org).

The lamp artist must carefully study each sheet of art glass to identify the portion that will best interpret a particular piece of pattern. Hand-rolled Tiffany reproduction glass comes in a wide variety of color combinations, and no two sheets are exactly the same.

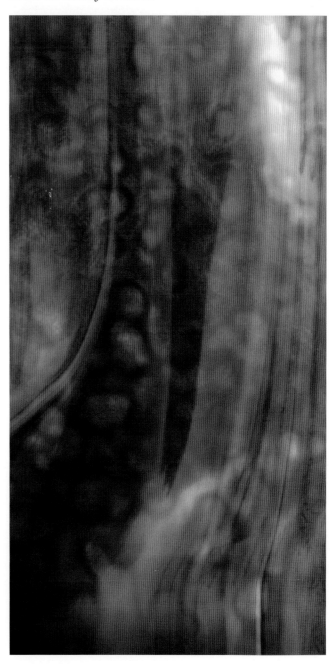

Our Glass Choices

For our **Elaborate Peony** project, we have selected the following art glass for the pattern pieces:

Flower petals (F): 1097RG, 1499RG, 5669RG, and UR00621

Leaves (L): 1431RG, 4403RG

Stems (S): UR0091

Borders (B): Oceana 303G

Background: NN637SP

Buds: Oceana 363

Bracts: 1499RG

Flower center (C): Laburnum B-RG

What Is Art Glass?

Art glass is 65 to 75 percent melted sand (silica), 15 to 20 percent an alkali base (usually potash or soda ash), and 10 to 15 percent lime, as well as color added through the use of inorganic (metallic) oxides. Each color or combination of colors produces a different cutability (the ease with which the glass scores or breaks), sheen, and color enhancement. Each also has a unique formula generally known only by the manufacturer. Red art glass, often considered specialty glass, is typically produced from gold, selenium, or copper, or a combination of these metallic oxides. It has an especially wide variety of appearances and is often the most expensive.

Two types of art glass are available to the lamp artist: hand-rolled Tiffany reproduction art glass and machine-produced art glass. Hand-rolled Tiffany art glass is manually ladled in molten form from the glass kiln, rolled by hand and mixed to disperse color, then flattened into an individual sheet, no two of which are alike. The machine-produced glass is made almost completely by machinery (of course), which has the mix formula programmed in and so creates a consistent final product, which is less expensive than hand-rolled glass.

Hand-rolled glass comes in an almost limitless variety of appearances, but because it can vary so much from sheet to sheet it can be difficult for the artist to know what they are getting unless they actually see the glass they're buying. Nevertheless, it is the hand-rolled Tiffany reproduction glass that offers the most vibrant colors, affording the artist the medium that is necessary to produce a museum-quality authentic reproduction lampshade.

Art glass is further divided into two general groups: opalescent and cathedral (or translucent). Opalescent art glass diffuses artificial or natural light, allowing its colors to glow when the glass is lit. Hand-rolled Tiffany reproduction art glass is most often always opalescent glass. Cathedral glass is transparent or translucent; because it often results in glaring "hot spots" when lit by a bulb, it is not considered suitable for Tiffany reproduction shades. (Interestingly, some authentic Tiffany shades do feature cathedral glass in the backgrounds; the hot spots caused by this are often obvious and detract from the value of the piece.)

Today there are only a handful of glass manufacturers that still produce hand-rolled Tiffany reproduction art glass: Youghigheny Opalescence (which also makes Oceana art glass), in Pennsylvania; Uroboros Glass and Bullseye Glass Company, in Oregon; Kokomo Opalescent Glass, in Indiana; and Chicago Art Glass, in Wisconsin. Each manufacturer generally produces a range of styles and textures of hand-rolled art glass—mottled, multicolor opals, rippled, herringbone, granite, and draperies—all of which are of use to the Tiffany lamp artist.

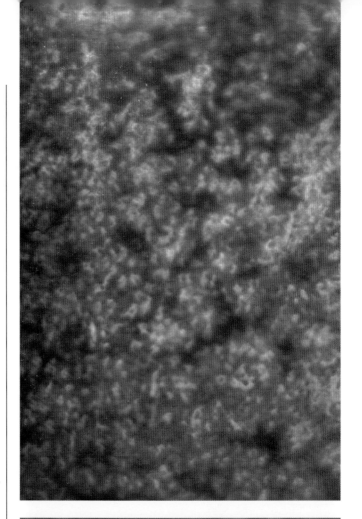

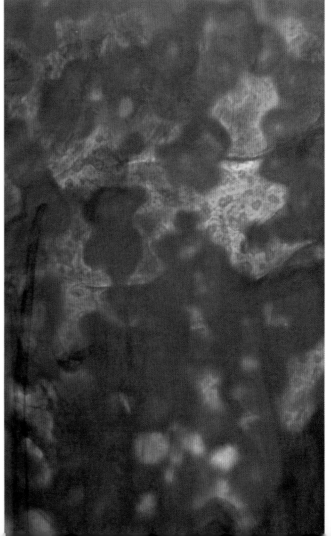

Expressing Nature Through Glass

We cannot overemphasize the need for you to take the time to carefully select the right glass for your shade. The selection of the most appropriate glass texture, color, density, and color "flow" becomes the pallet the lamp artist uses to best represent a personal expression of an actual flower or other figurative image. While the reproduction lamp mold kit provides a Tiffany peony flower pattern, the artist needs to have the peony's specific coloring and appearance in mind so the flower can be accurately and evocatively represented. The best way to do this is to learn about and study the real thing.

The peony is a perennial flowering plant or shrub with several hybrid versions and colors, the principal colors being white, yellow, and varying shades of red. It is a traditional floral symbol of China and the state flower of Indiana. Louis Comfort Tiffany represented the peony in a number of his art-glass shades; it is perhaps his most widely depicted flower.

An examination of real peonies shows that the flower-petal color goes from its deepest at the base of the flower to a lighter shade towards the edge of the petal. Peony buds are typically a consistent deep color throughout.

Choosing Individual Pieces

Selecting the right sheets of art glass for a shade is just the first step, however. A light table is needed to help the lamp artist carefully select specific areas of the sheet that will best represent the flower's color variations, shadings (where leaves or flower petals overlap), and grain directions. We glue the cut-out pattern pieces to the glass with rubber cement, using the light table to let us see the best position for paper pieces.

It might be tempting at this point to squeeze as many pattern pieces as you can onto a glass sheet so as to use as much of the glass as possible. Avoid this temptation. Your guiding principle should be to find the area of glass that best represents what you have in mind for a particular piece. Look closely at the subtle color variations, the grain of the glass, the darkness or brightness and select the portion that will work best, even if it means using a relatively small portion of a sheet. (You can, of course, save the unused portions for other patterns.)

Breaking, Grinding, and Foiling

After we position and glue the pattern pieces, the art glass is cut out around the pattern and ground to remove the rough edges and carefully match the paper pattern. The paper pattern is removed and the glass tile is soaked in a mild commercial cleaner solution (Simple Green works well for this) to loosen grit. We then scrub the edges of the glass to make sure the edges are clean for

The best way to plan a color scheme and select glass for a floral pattern is to look at live flowers and buds. Here, a variety of peony blossoms reveal the various colors and intensities the lamp artist should strive to reproduce.

foiling. It is then wise to write the pattern piece number on each tile with a waterproof marker for easy identification, using the intact pattern as a reference. (Note: The Elaborate Peony pattern does not identify buds and bracts separately, so we have identified and marked the buds and bracts, as we are using a different art glass to represent these.)

The next step is to dry and foil each piece with $^3/_8$-inch copper foil. Careful cleaning of the tile edges will help ensure that the foil adheres properly. We use $^3/_8$-inch foil, as it provides a sufficiently thin lead line around the small tiles.

The inspired lamp artist might want to create foil strips using the same method Tiffany used. This technique involves waxing the back of a 1 millimeter thick soft copper sheet and slicing it into suitable strips. Some artists still use this labor-intensive technique today.

We recommend that you keep the foiled tiles sorted, keeping all the pieces needed to make one repeat separated from the others. Doing so will make it easier to assemble the pattern on the mold. You might also want to test-fit individual flowers on the mylar pattern, using the light table, to make certain of a good fit and that you are satisfied with the color selection and grain direction.

Once foiled, the individual glass tiles are ready for assembly on the fiberglass mold as described in chapter 4, beginning on page 32.

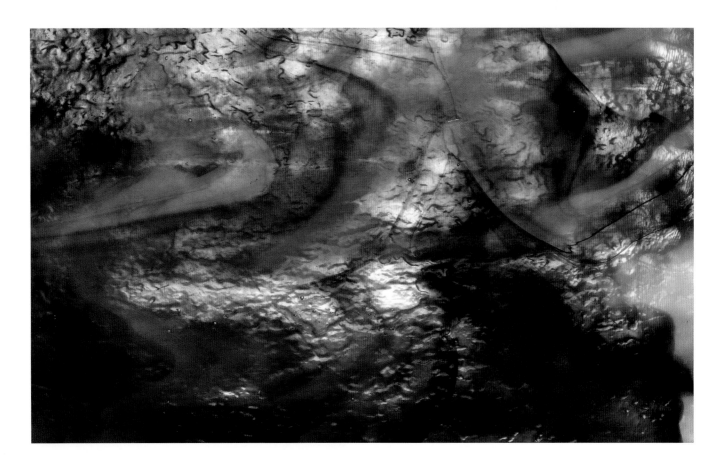

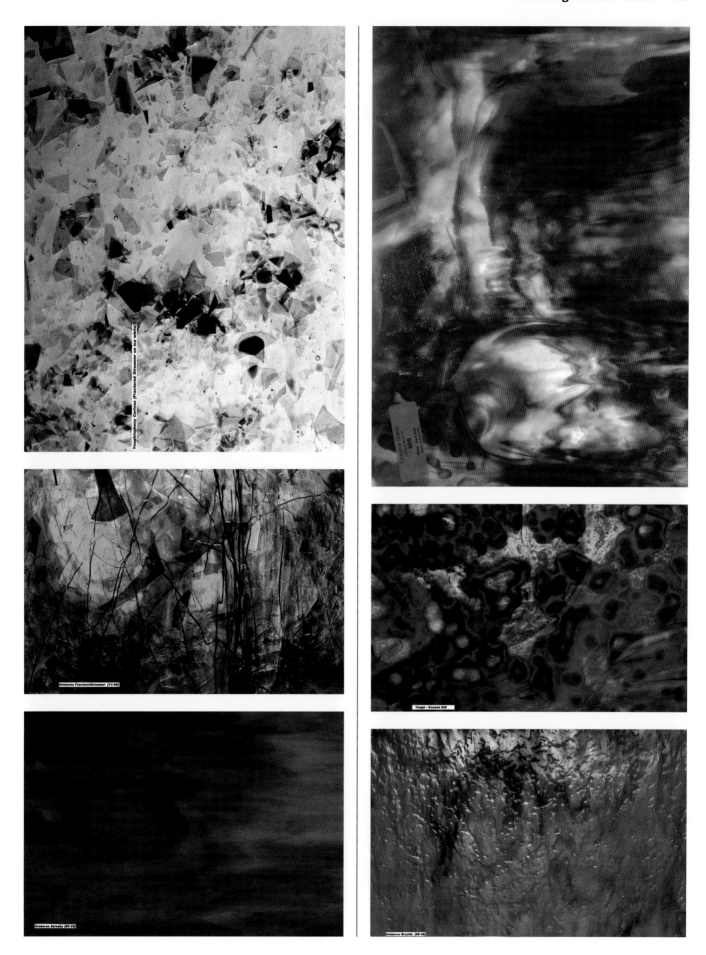

Youghiogheny Carious (Fractured Streamer on ice white)

Uroboros Fracture/Streamer [11-84]

Uroboros Streaky [60-33]

Oceana Glass 605

Yough - Oceana 628

Uroboros Granite [60-16]

12-inch Dogwood on a Lace base

16-inch Woodbine on a Small Stick base

**16-inch Banded Daffodil on an original
Handel base, with details**

15-inch Spider on a Mushroom base

16-inch Turtleback Band on a Turtleback base

16-inch Dragonfly on a Snake and Basket base, with details

16-inch Daffodil on a blown-glass Flask base, with details

16-inch Pansy on a
blown-glass Vial base,
with details

18-inch Clematis on a Stick
base, with details

16-inch Dogwood on a Mock Turtle base

20-inch Waterlily on a Cattail and Pond Lily base

4. Assembling the Tiles

For the first-time reproduction-lamp builder, it would be advisable, after your glass selection has been made, to break, grind, clean, foil, and assemble one complete repeat of your project so that you can evaluate and, if necessary, make changes to your glass selection. This should be done before all the shade's tiles are cut.

To create a "test" repeat, we used a light table and a piece of clear, double-strength glass or a $^1/_{16}$-inch-thick clear plastic laminate. A pattern copy of the repeat was taped to the light table and the clear double-strength glass was laid on top of the copy. The individual foiled tiles were then affixed to the overlaying glass in their respective positions using rubber cement. This dry run will ensure that the artist is completely satisfied with the glass selection and positioning before the entire shade is assembled and soldered.

Working with Wax

When the fit is established, we use Odyssey Tacky Wax to affix the glass tiles to the mold. The wax is melted in a suitable Crock-Pot then carefully applied, just a small touch, to the backside of a foiled tile using a flux brush. The melted wax can also be applied to the corresponding mold area. The tile is then pressed into place on the mold.

The mold comes with a recessed area at the top designed to take the brass aperture ring. The ring should be centered in the recessed area; the tiles forming the first border row, at the aperture, are then set one by one against the ring. We begin assembling the glass pieces on the mold starting at the aperture and working around the mold and downwards toward the bottom rim.

Because we cut away all the black lines on the paper copies of the pattern, the foiled tiles placed on the mold might have some space between them, which is not unusual. The wax allows slight movement of each tile's position, and so it is easy at this point to adjust the individual pieces on the mold in order to provide an equal separation between them. This way, the lead lines on the soldered mold will be a consistent width. A fair amount of adjustment is needed as well because the tiles are flat but the mold is rounded. Remember that the

Cut, ground, and foiled tiles are ready to be assembled on the mold. The $^3/_8$ foil used here creates a thin solder line and is standard for authentic reproduction Tiffany shades. The more precisely you apply the foil, the more even the lead lines on the finished piece will be.

grout lines on the mold are intended to serve as guidelines for tile placement before tinning the shade. When assembly is complete, the ring is removed.

Dealing with a Tucked Rim

Just like the original Tiffany shade, the 22-inch Elaborate Peony features what's called a tucked rim (the diameter of the rim is less than the diameter across the largest section of the mold; i.e., the rim curves inward). This requires that the shade be set up in two separate sections; otherwise, you will not be able to release the shade from the mold after it has been tinned. We have delineated an untinned break line that generally follows the top of the second border row of tiles at the bottom of the shade, which is approximately where the shade is at its widest. This line remains untinned as you tin the entire outer shade above and below the line.

Odyssey Tacky Wax is formulated to securely hold tiles on the mold even during the soldering process. Standard paraffin or candle wax won't work.

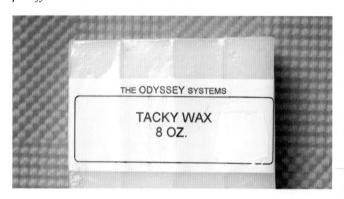

Tile assembly is the satisfying process of making what seems like a disorganized set of hundreds (or thousands) of glass tiles gradually come together as a beautiful shade.

The best way to melt the wax is to use a small Crock-Pot (while Tacky Wax is not harmful, it's probably best to use the Crock-Pot only for wax). An 8-ounce package of wax is divided into four individual bars; a large shade like the 22-inch Elaborate Peony will take no more than two bars. Unused melted and rehardened wax can be remelted and used for other molds.

Before any tiles are assembled on the mold, make certain you have the proper size brass ring for the aperture. The 22-inch Elaborate Peony shade takes a 5-inch ring.

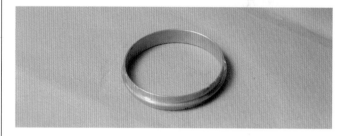

Assemble the tiles starting at the top of the mold.

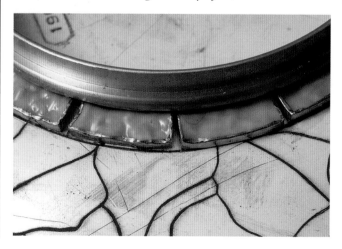

Apply melted wax to the back of a foiled tile and the mold using a flux brush or similar small bristle-brush. Synthetic or "sponge" brushes will melt in the hot wax and so cannot be used. Set the glass tiles into place on the mold, centering them within the grout lines.

The first row of border tiles are set around the aperture (after this is done, the ring is set on the top of the mold with the large flange pointing down).

Place each waxed tile into position around the aperture, making sure they are seated up to the edge of the opening.

Tile position can be adjusted even after the tile is affixed to the mold.

If you've cut and ground the tiles carefully, each piece should fit in place with a little adjustment. Remember that the incised lines on the mold function only as guidelines for placement (the outlines on the patterns are what should be used to cut and shape each tile).

Notice how the tiles around the aperture go underneath the ring's overhang.

It might help to check the tiles on the pattern before you apply them to the mold. That way you'll be sure your glass tiles match the pattern.

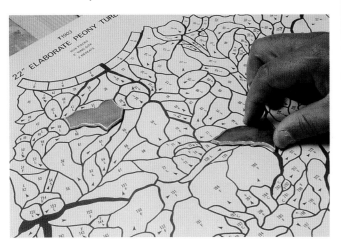

Continue to assemble the tiles by applying a bit of melted wax to the mold and the back of the tile and pressing the piece into place.

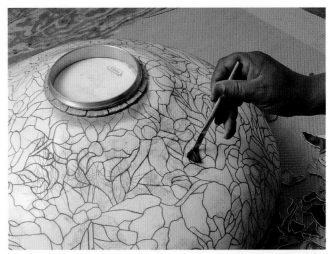

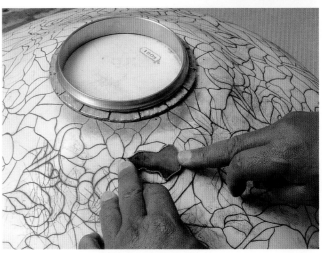

As you assemble, the pattern emerges. Remember that because the tiles were cut by hand, not by a machine, there will always be slight irregularities in their outlines, and small gaps between the pieces are not unusual. As well, because the tiles are flat and the mold is rounded, the tiles will not lay perfectly level; larger pieces should be set so that the center of the tile sits flat on the mold with both ends slightly raised.

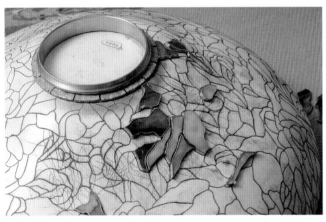

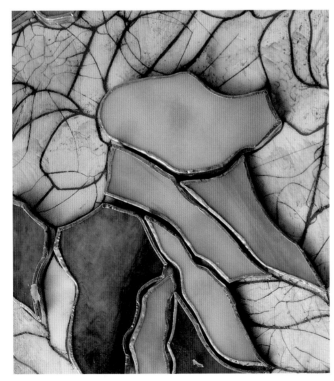

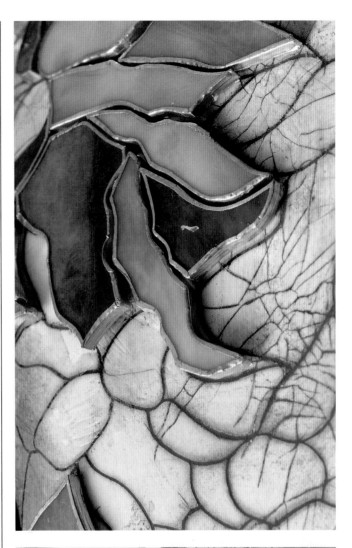

When all the tiles are assembled, the shade is ready for tinning, except for the rim . . .

This image shows the line that separates the shade into two sections (we've left the bottom section only partially assembled). Use a marker to make indicator marks above and below the perimeter of the line to help you position the two sections when it comes time to join them together.

Tin the top section of the shade and the bottom section separately, leaving a continuous line between the two sections untinned. (Tiffany molds that don't have a tucked rim can be tinned all at one time.)

. . . the Elaborate Peony shade has a "tucked rim"—the bottom opening is narrower than the broadest part of the shade—and so cannot be fully tinned until the shade is released from the mold in two sections. The shade is left untinned along a continuous joint that goes all the way around the shade at its widest point. If this line were tinned, the shade could not be removed from the mold.

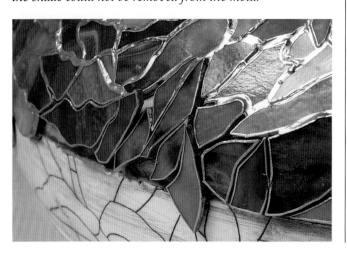

At this point, the shade is ready to be released from the mold.

5. Releasing the Shade

Once we have completed tinning the two separate sections of the tucked-rim peony shade, we are now ready to release the shade from the fiberglass mold. While it's still on the mold, the shade is marked with a Sharpie at three locations at roughly equal distances around the circumference, above and below the break line. This will help ensure that when we reassemble the two sections, after removal from the mold, they will be fitted together properly.

To heat the outside of the lampshade and melt the wax, we use a Wagner Power Stripper, a tool intended to help refinishers strip wallpaper. You can also use a crafter's heat gun for this job, or even a hair dryer set on high, but remember that the less heat the tool generates, the longer it will take to soften the wax sufficiently (because of this, a hair dryer is suitable only for small shades). If you do use a power stripper, which we have found does the job best, always wear a pair of heat-resistant gloves, which will also help you to handle the heated lamp shade.

Another way to melt the wax is to heat the shade (if it's not too big) in an oven set at around 200 degrees. If this method is used, the shade should be carefully monitored so it doesn't get too hot and the glass tiles crack.

It takes about 15 to 20 minutes for a power stripper to melt the wax enough to release the shade. When it does, the section below the break line will separate and start to fall away from the top section. At this point, we turn the shade over and remove the lower section first, followed by the top section. While the released shade is still hot, we use a heavy-duty paper towel to remove as much wax from the inside of the shade as we can. (We will clean off all the wax more thoroughly at a later stage).

The Ring and Reassembly

The next step is to attach the 5-inch aperture ring. To do this, we place the ring on a flat, level surface with the long flange facing upward. We then fit the aperture of the shade over the flange and solder the ring to the upper section of the inside of the shade. Different size Tiffany shades require different size aperture rings; the specific diameter required for each shade, from 2 inches to 6 inches, is printed on the shade's pattern.

If you use a power stripper, keep the nozzle at least a few inches from the shade and move it around so one spot doesn't get overheated. Wear protective gloves when heating the shade; the gun and the glass will get quite hot.

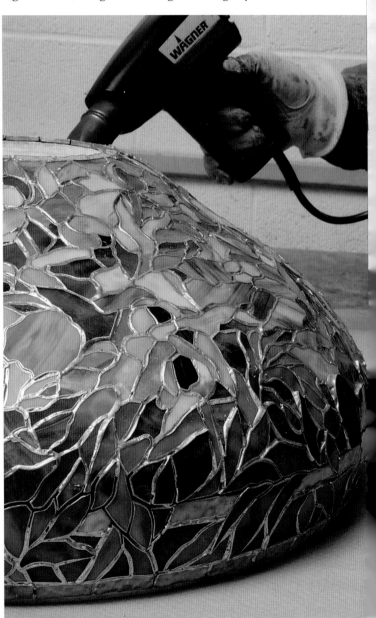

It is now time to refit the lower section of the shade to the upper section, matching up the three marks we made before releasing the shade from the mold. This must be done carefully to avoid breaking off any protruding tiles. Once the upper and lower sections are properly aligned, we tack-solder at points on the break line all the way around the circumference of the shade.

The shade is then turned on its side to allow the break line to be positioned horizontally. You can do this with help from a lamp jig or a set of Wedgies. The entire break line is then tinned on the inside of the shade.

Here a power stripper is used to heat up the wax sufficiently so it releases its grip on the glass. Depending on the heat source, melting the wax could take a fair amount of time—20 to 30 minutes at least. The mold itself is manufactured to withstand the heat.

As the wax melts, the lower section of the shade will begin to drop away from the upper section along the untinned line. Apply the heat for a few more minutes, and the shade should be ready to come off the mold.

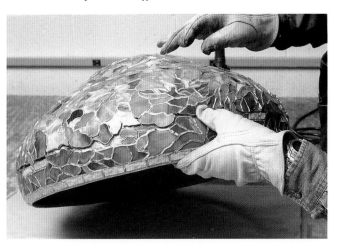

Pull the mold up and away from the top section of the shade. If it doesn't release fairly easily, you might need to apply more heat.

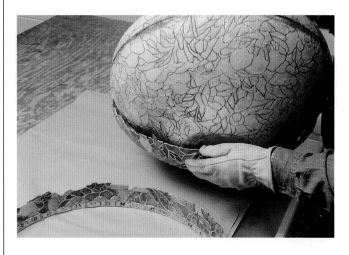

When the two pieces are finally free, set the mold aside.

While the shade is still warm, wipe off as much wax as you can from the inside with a piece of heavy-duty paper towel. Wax remover will be used later to clean the shade more thoroughly.

Occasionally a tile or two may come loose as the shade is released. Make any necessary repairs at this point.

The just-released shade is reasonably sturdy, but be careful not to bump it or handle it roughly.

The next step is to attach the aperture ring to the shade from the inside. Flux and solder each joint that touches the ring.

The two shade sections need to be reassembled.

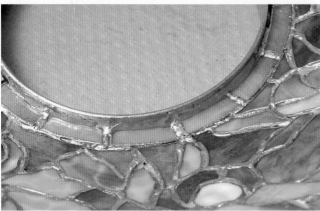

Carefully place the lower section on top of the upside-down upper section, matching up the indicator marks you made earlier.

The sections should fit together with a bit of adjustment. Use caution, however, so you don't accidentally break off any protruding tiles.

When the sections are properly positioned, they can be tack-soldered together.

Tack-solder along the untinned line, carefully working your way around the entire shade.

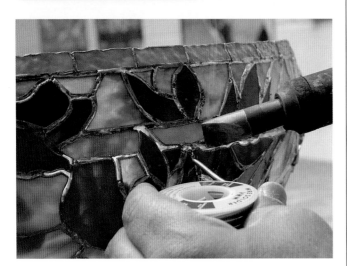

When you finish tack-soldering the outside of the shade, fully tin the untinned line on the inside of the shade.

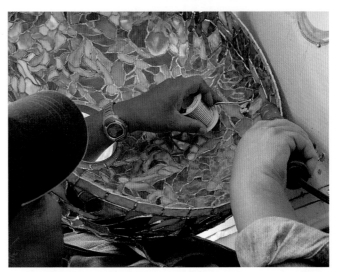

6. Attaching the Rim

The shade is now ready to have a $^3/_{16}$-inch rim attached to its lower edge. This rim thickness is standard for all reproductions, many of which need a rim for reinforcement. The shade is turned upside down on a flat, level surface. The rim is set all along the lower edge and held in place with binder clips. A properly sized rim will be approximately 2 or 3 inches longer than what is necessary for the shade and will need to be trimmed.

Beginning at approximately the center of one of the lower border tiles, we place binder clips 3 to 5 inches apart all around the bottom to hold the rim in place. As we do this, we allow the rim to find its natural level—do not use the clips to force the rim into contact with the bottom edge along its entire length. Doing so will result in an uneven final edge. There will be spots where there is a gap between the rim and the bottom and places where there is no gap. The gaps are simply filled with solder, ensuring a flat and level lower edge.

With the shade still upside down, we completely flux the rim and the area between the rim and lower border tiles. Beginning at the first spacing, between two clips, we apply the tip of the soldering iron to the rim until the rim gets hot enough to melt the solder, and then apply solder along the rim to the next clamp. The solder will flow down and fill the area between the rim and the lower border tiles.

We attach the rim to the lower edge in this manner until we reach a point that it becomes necessary to trim the excess length of rim. We mark the overlap end of the rim approximately $^1/_{16}$ inch beyond where the initial end is attached. Then we use a hacksaw or bolt cutter to cut off the extra length of rim. We align the two ends of the rim, clip them in place, then complete the soldering, filling in any gap between the rim tips.

This large shade will require reinforcement to strengthen it. The $^3/_{16}$-inch brass rim will be added all the way around the lower edge of the shade, and reinforcing wire will be placed in three places on the inside of the shade from the aperture to the rim.

The rim, a piece of $^3/_{16}$-inch-diameter copper wire about 72 inches long (a good 2 or 3 inches longer than the shade's lower 69-inch circumference), is set on top of the shade's lower edge while the shade is upside-down and held in place with binder clips. The rim begins in the center of a lower border tile; it must not have any kinks or bends.

45

The rim shouldn't follow every little contour of the lower edge—it should be allowed to "level itself" as it goes around the shade. If you force the rim tight against the glass tiles and hold it in place with a clip, the rim will be uneven after it's attached.

A clip every 5 or 6 inches should suffice to hold the rim in place.

The ends of the rim will overlap at this point.

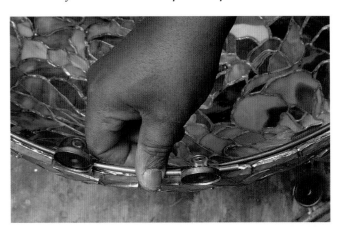

Beginning at the rim's starting point, flux and tack-solder the rim to the bottom of the shade every couple of inches. Fluxing between the rim and the lower border tiles and applying heat and solder to the rim will allow the solder to be drawn in to the space between the rim and tiles.

Then tin and solder the entire rim, removing the clips as you go.

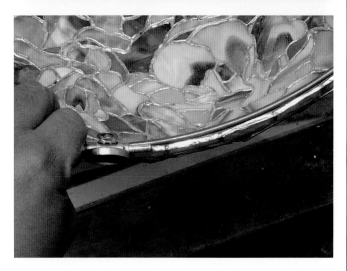

Smooth out any bumps you make with the soldering iron.

When you approach the end of the rim, make a mark just where it overlaps the other end.

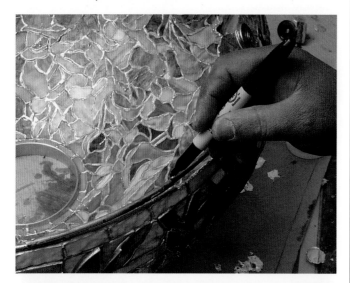

Solder the rim in place, then fill any gap with a bit of solder. The rim reinforcement will provide a clean edge to the bottom of the shade and strengthen the entire piece considerably. You'll also want to add reinforcing copper wire at three spots inside the shade. Instructions for doing this are offered in chapter 7, beginning on page 70.

Cut the rim at the mark.

24-inch Rosebush on a Perforated base, with details

18-inch Nasturtium Turban on a Library base, with details

20-inch Poppy Cone on a Twisted Vine base, with details

16-inch Poinsettia on a Small Lion's Paw base

18-inch Grapevine on a Large Tree Trunk base

18-inch Trumpet Vine on a Large
Tree Trunk base, with details

**18-inch Wisteria Vine on a Large
Tree Trunk base, with details**

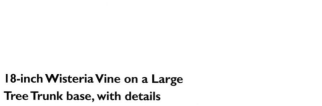

20-inch Poppy Cone on a blown-glass
Crab base, with details

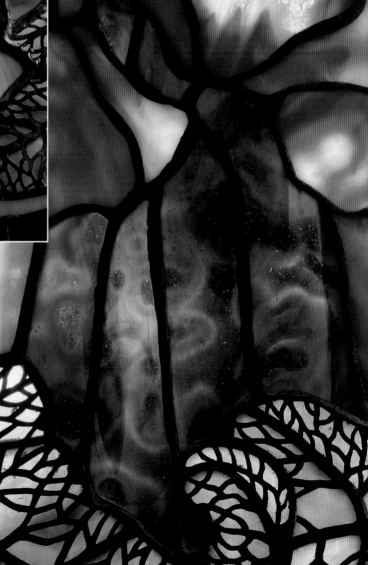

18-inch Tulip Dome on a Library base

22-inch Nasturtium Turban on a Root base

22-inch Laburnum on a Bird Skeleton
base, with details

18-inch Cobweb and Apple
Blossom on a Wheat Mosaic
base, with details

7. Reinforcing the Shade

All lampshades 22 inches or more in diameter should be reinforced on the inside using 12-gauge solid soft copper wire (you can buy this ready to use, or strip 12-gauge copper electrical wiring). We will install three reinforcing wires, which will generally follow the line between the three repeats of the Elaborate Peony pattern. We first place the reinforcing wire on the inside of the shade at the aperture ring where the ring is met by the lead line along the edge of one of the repeats. About 1/4 inch of the wire is set against and soldered to the ring. From there the wire will follow the lead line down to the rim. As we position and solder the wire in place, we make sure it is laid in the center of the lead line. Should the wire fall outside of the line, it will be visible on the outside of the shade when the lamp is lit.

After three reinforcing wires are affixed on the inside of the shade, the piece is completely tinned and bead-soldered on the inside. During the soldering of the inside of the lampshade, excess wax is often melted and begins to drip; it should be removed promptly. The shade is then reversed and the outside surface is beaded. After the lamp is completely beaded, outside and inside, a signature plate is attached to the rim. Artists should always sign their work to prevent it from being represented as an unsigned original.

The lower edge of the shade is then sanded smooth with a handheld electric rotary sander, first with a 60-grit pad and then a finer 100-grit pad. Both the bottom and the sides of the rim should be sanded.

Next we go over the inside of the shade with the power stripper and remove all the remaining wax using paper towels. We then apply a citrus-based cleaning solution (such as Goof Off) with an abrasive pad to remove any remaining wax as well as any markings that still remain on the tiles. The shade is then thoroughly scrubbed with a solution of Simple Green and water. It is now ready to be sent to a professional electroplater to be copper plated.

The first reinforcing wire should begin at the aperture ring and follow a soldered seam to the bottom of the shade.

70

Lay the tip of the wire on the ring so it overlaps by about ¹/₄ inch and runs along a soldered seam.

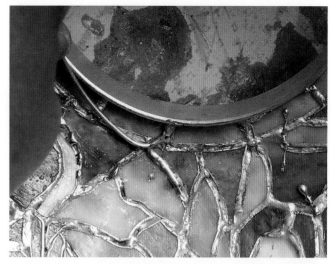

Hold it in place with the tip of a pair of needle-nose pliers.

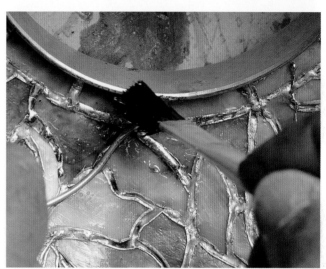

Tack the copper wire to the ring and the seam. This can be a bit tricky; to do it, you need to hold the pliers with one hand while using the other hand to handle the soldering iron—picking up some solder and tacking the wire in one motion.

Continue working your way toward the rim, bending the wire to follow a seam and fluxing and tacking it in place.

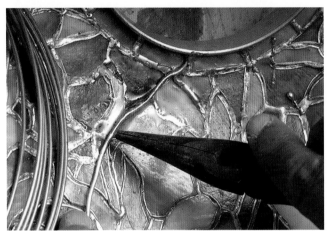

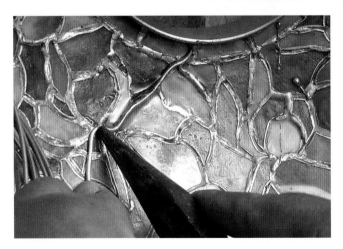

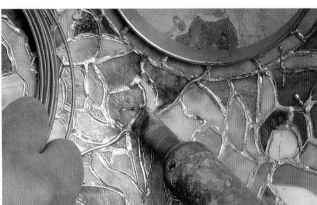

Be careful to keep the wire on a seam; don't let it run over any glass or it will be visible from the other side when the shade is lit.

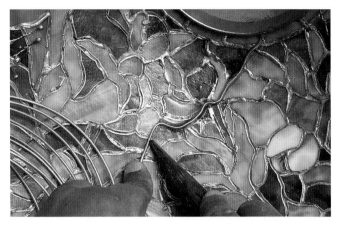

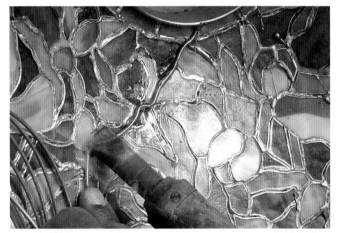

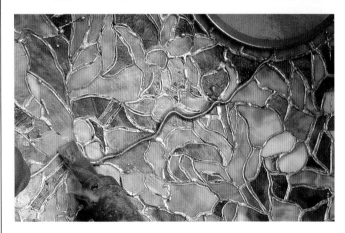

The copper wire will provide good support to the shade, allowing it to maintain its shape when handled.

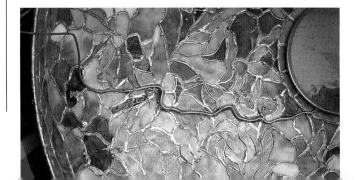

It doesn't really matter which seam you follow so long as it is continuous from aperture ring to bottom rim.

When you reach the bottom of the shade, trim the wire and solder the end so it is attached just shy of the edge of the bottom rim. You don't want the wire to extend beyond the bottom of the shade. When the wire rib is tacked in place, go back and solder it completely.

Two more reinforcing wires are recommended for this 22-inch shade.

All artists should sign their work. The artist attaches a personalized brass plate to the inside of each shade he or she creates, just above the rim.

To attach the plate, set it in place, with its ends lying against a seam.

Then flux and solder one end of the plate to the closest seam.

Do the same for the other side.

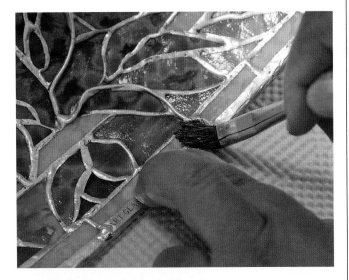

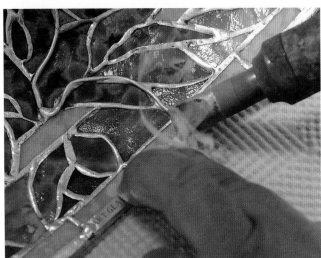

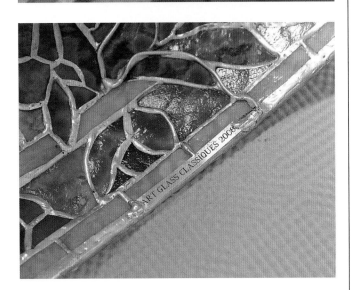

Then solder the edge of the plate along the rim.

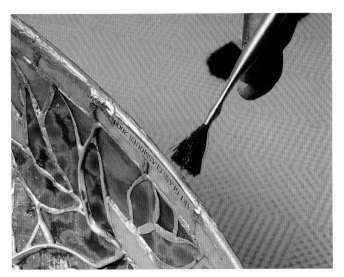

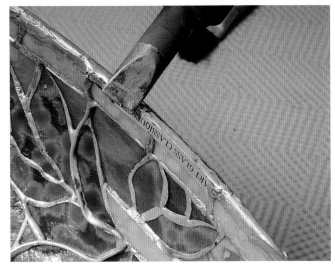

The final step in the construction of the shade is to sand the rim. We'll use two different sandpapers—a fairly coarse 60 grit, followed by a 100 grit, both for metal—and a small hand sander.

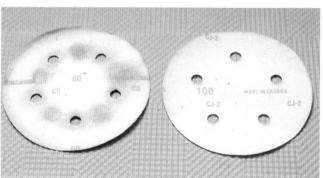

Run the sander along the bottom of the rim to smooth it and remove any burrs.

Sand the inside and outside of the rim, too.

The sanded surface should be smooth to the touch.

Working With Filigree

Several Tiffany lamp patterns, including the well-known Dragonfly, make use of brass filigree over the tiles. We will demonstrate how to prepare and attach filigree for the 16-inch Dragonfly shade, since it is so popular, but the techniques are basically the same for every filigree pattern.

Dragonfly filigree wings come in sets of four, representing one insect's four separate wings. Because the Dragonfly pattern has seven repeats, a total of seven sets of wings are needed for the 16-inch shade. The filigree set is cut apart, using sheet-metal shears, with care being taken to completely trim off the connecting pieces without damaging the brass work.

We then match the individual filigree wing overlays to a copy of the pattern sheet and mark them using a black Sharpie where they have to be cut to match the glass tile that they will cover. The filigree is then carefully cut along these marks, and the position is rechecked on the pattern.

When soldering the filigree in place over the respective wing tile, care should be taken not to fill the holes in the filigree with solder. The filigree piece is held onto the glass wing tile and flux applied only to the edge to be soldered. The two edges, the filigree and glass tile, should then be soldered, using a very small amount of solder, as if you want to only tin the edge.

The popular 16-inch Tiffany Dragonfly shade features brass filigree that represents the insects' wings. The pattern indicates where the wings appear to overlap.

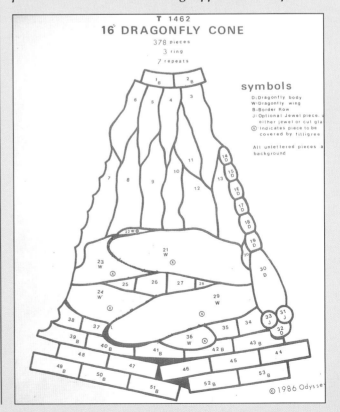

The filigree is applied on top of the respective glass tiles and tin-soldered into place to ensure that no excess solder fills the openings. To accomplish this, the overlapped wings must be cut into pieces—the filigree doesn't actually overlap.

The wings are sold in sets of four—one set for each of the seven dragonflies on the shade. Use metal shears to carefully cut apart each separate wing.

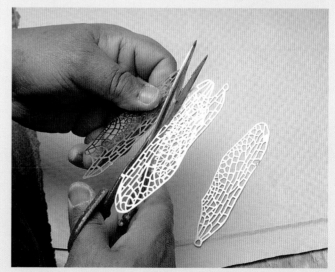

Place on the pattern one of the wings that is overlapped by another.

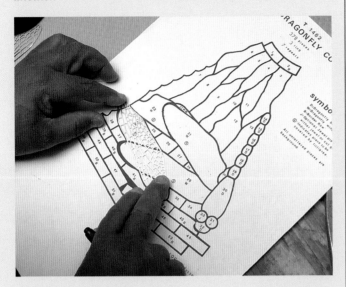

Use a marker to draw lines on the wing where the overlaps occur.

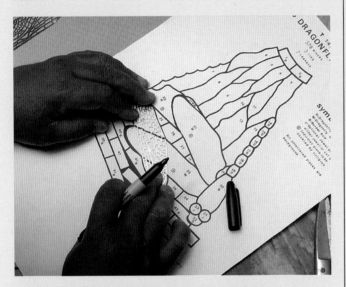

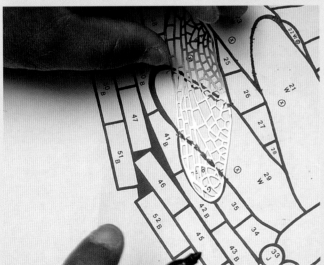

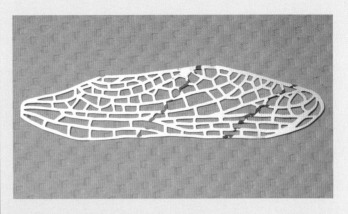

Carefully cut the wing apart along the lines. Do the same for the insect's other overlapped wing.

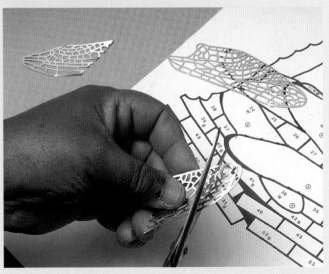

Check the fit by placing the two overlapped and two uncut overlapping wings on the pattern.

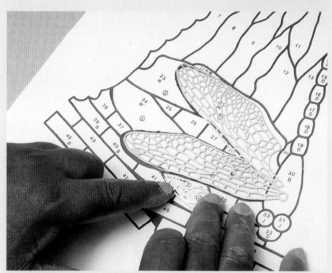

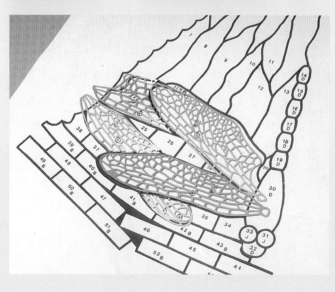

Notice that traditionally both wings on one side of the dragonfly are overlapped by the wings on one side of the adjacent dragonfly—no single dragonfly has both sets of wings overlapping both insects next it. The Tiffany Poppy pattern also makes use of filigree, which is prepared in a similar manner.

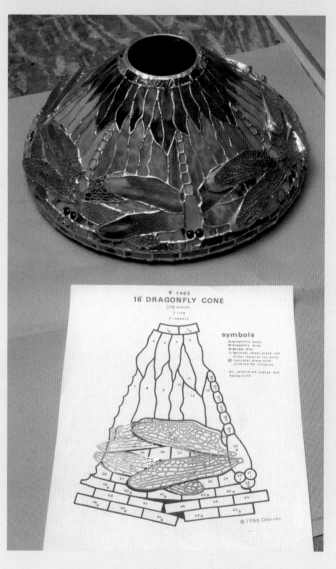

8. Applying a Patina and Finishing

While the art glass that you select for your reproduction lampshade is the most critical component of the project, a good final patina is crucial to how well your finished shade actually looks like an authentic Tiffany piece.

There are a number of commercial patinas on the market, but no matter which patina you choose, having your shade copper-plated by a good commercial plater before you apply the patina will ensure that the finish will look authentic. The patina needs a sufficiently thick copper base for it to take well—obtaining this base can be accomplished only through electroplating.

We will be using our own patina mixes for the 22-inch Elaborate Peony shade in order to create an authentic verde-green on a red-brown ground. In our opinion, this mixture works better than any commercial patina on the market. Our patinas are prepared with chemicals purchased from a laboratory supplier in keeping with the following formulae:

Verde-Green

    Copper sulfate: 8 ounces
    Ammonium Chloride: 4 ounces
    Sodium Chloride: 4 ounces
    Zinc Chloride: 1 ounce
    Acetic Acid: 2 ounces
    Mix with 1 gallon of deionized water.

Red-Brown

    Copper (cupric) nitrate: 7 ounces
    Sodium chloride: 7 ounces
    Mix with 34 fluid ounces (1 liter) of deionized water.

The Patina Process

When the shade comes back from the plater, it is best to "age" the plating by waiting at least 7 days before any patina is applied. Should the plating job appear to be spotty or thin in some places, we apply several coatings of JAX Copper Plating Solution to these areas, allowing

The chemicals needed to make the patina formula are available in small quantities from online laboratory supply houses. They must be handled with utmost care.

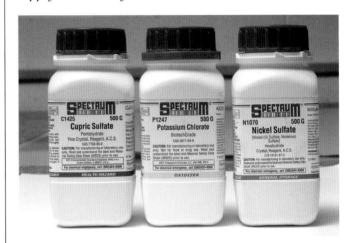

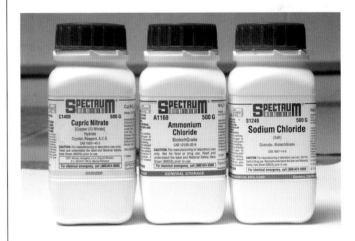

the shade to air dry between each coating. After the final coat, we allow the shade to sit and age for at least 7 days.

The verde patina is applied first to the "aged" lampshade as it is more unstable and difficult to work with than the red-brown. Always apply patina in a well-lit and well-ventilated room, and always wear chemical-resistant gloves. We apply the verde patina to the entire outer and inner surfaces of the shade using a water-dampened sponge, then allow the shade to sit for 15 to 20 minutes. We then rinse the shade in cold water, pat it dry with a clean towel, and let it sit for 1 to 2 hours before applying the red-brown patina.

The Second Color

The red-brown sometimes takes a little time to set up properly, based on the quality and thickness of the copper plating. We apply the red-brown patina once and watch to see if it takes well to the copper plate—this is indicated by a cloudy, reddish coloring of the metal. If it does, we apply 1 or 2 more coats over a 2- to 3-day period. Each coat is allowed to sit for 15 to 20 minutes, rinsed in cold water, placed wet in a black plastic garbage bag, and stored for 24 hours, until the next day's coating. It's important that too much red-brown patina not be applied at any one time as this will result in the development of a black color and all the patina will have to be removed and reapplied. (Should the patina have to be removed, allow the shade to sit for another 7 to 10 days to age before reapplying the new patina.)

After the final coating of red-brown, the shade is again allowed to sit for 15 to 20 minutes, rinsed in cold water, again placed wet in the black plastic garbage bag and stored for approximately 10 more days.

The shade is then removed from the bag, thoroughly cleaned with Simple Green or a similar cleaner to remove any residual patina, and finished with a paste wax or flat-matte or low-gloss lacquer, which provides a final finish. While not necessary, we have found that this final finish gives a welcome shine to the piece and protects the carefully created patina.

Commercial Patinas

If you don't want to order and mix your own patinas, you can use commercially available ready-made ones. To do so, carefully follow the directions on the patina bottles. We've applied JAX patinas—green first, followed by red-brown—using a toothbrush as directed. After the first application, the piece is allowed to sit for 15 minutes while the green patina sets. Then the piece is rinsed in cold water and allowed to air dry. The brown patina is then applied, allowed to set for 15 minutes, rinsed in cold water, and allowed to air dry.

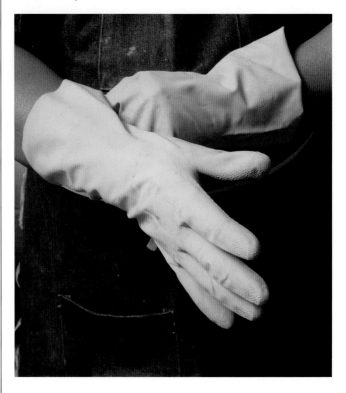

Wear chemical-protective gloves when mixing chemicals and applying a patina, and always work in a well-ventilated space.

The verde-green mixture is applied first. It can be applied with a small sponge.

Choosing a Base

Lamp bases are an important part of an authentic reproduction lamp. They are crucial to properly support the sometimes very heavy lampshade. They should also complement the shade: They should be the appropriate height, shape, and style to properly display the shade. The base should not be so ornate that it detracts from the beauty of the shade. Selecting the proper base is almost as important as selecting the art glass that makes up the shade.

Lamp bases suitable for reproduction Tiffany shades come in a variety of sizes and shapes, most of which are interpretations, although some are exact reproductions of original Tiffany bases. Almost all of these reproduction bases are made of brass/bronze and are given an antique brown-green patina or are painted to generally match the shade's patina.

There are two commercial sources of reproduction bases available to the lamp reproduction artist: Source One and Odyssey. Source One bases, all solid brass/bronze, are interpretations of original Tiffany designs and are painted instead of having a patina. The final finish is rather rough, but the bases are relatively inexpensive. They can be a good choice for a beginning lamp artist's efforts.

Odyssey carries two lines of reproduction bases: the LB and WB lines. The first is a line of authentic reproduction bases (except for the modern light switch) featuring patterns taken directly from original Tiffany bases. These LB bases are handsomely finished with a green-brown patina. They are quite expensive, however. The less-expensive WB line of bases comprises interpretations of Tiffany originals.

At the extreme high end of the scale are authentic reproduction bases made by a handful of small lamp studios that repair authentic Tiffany bases and develop patterns using these originals. These reproductions can be remarkable; some are distinguishable from an original only by an expert. The time and effort involved in producing these reproductions make them quite costly, however, and so they are generally used by only a very small number of artists.

We have selected a Large Lion's Paw base for our finished 22-inch Elaborate Peony reproduction lamp shade, which nicely complements the reproduction. Our base is fitted with a 5-inch wheel, on which the shade sits, and a teardrop reproduction cap.

Starting on the inside of the shade, pour a small quantity of the chemical mixture into the shade.

Then use the sponge to spread the mixture over every soldered line.

Using a suitable base for your lampshade is an important part of the creative process. Choose a simpler style for simpler shades. Larger and more detailed shades can handle more ornate bases. While Tiffany patterns don't necessarily have only one style of base that will suit them, some patterns were often matched with a particular base. A little bit of research online or in the library or bookstore will help you determine what base might be appropriate for your pattern.

In general, there are two simple rules of thumb for selecting a base for a table lamp: The section of the base that rests on the table should not be larger in diameter than half the diameter of the shade. The height of the lamp base from its base to the wheel on which the shade sits should not be greater than one and a quarter times the diameter of the shade.

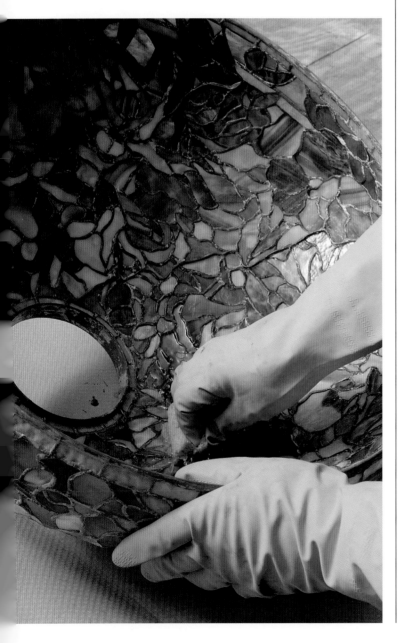

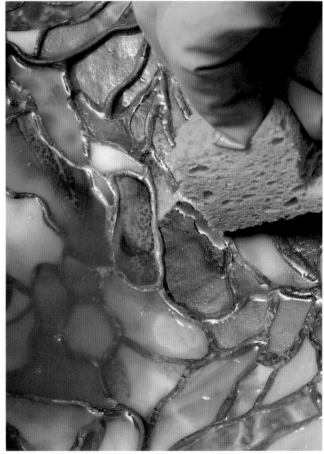

Use a fair amount of mixture to thoroughly cover all the lines. They will change color slightly right away; the change will increase as time passes.

Cover the entire shade, inside and out, as well as the ring and rim. The red-brown patina is applied in the same manner. Having your shade copper-plated by a professional plater before you apply a patina will result in a rich and authentic finish.

An authentic patina is an essential finishing touch to a museum-quality authentic reproduction Tiffany lamp.

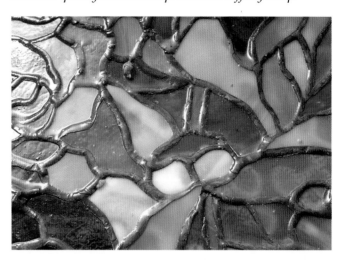

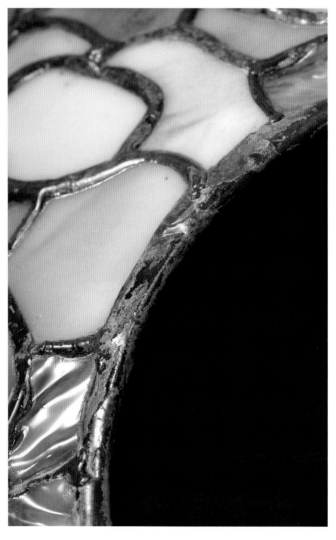

Shade Pattern and Base Model Numbers

12-inch Dogwood: 1417
   Lace base: 325
16-inch Woodbine: 1468
   Small Stick base: 533
16-inch Banded Daffodil: 1449R
15-inch Spider: 1424
   Mushroom Base: 337
16-inch Turtleback Band: 1434
   Turtleback base: 5086
16-inch Dragonfly: 1462
   Snake and Basket Base: 140
16-inch Daffodil: 1449
   Blown-glass Flask base: 338
16-inch Pansy: 1448
   Blown-glass Vial base: 21667
18-inch Clematis: 1480
   Stick base: 534
16-inch Dogwood: 1446
   Mock Turtle base: 587
20-inch Waterlily: 1490
   Cattail and Pond Lily base: 453

24-inch Rosebush: 1915
   Perforated base: 387
18-inch Nasturtium Turban: 1533
   Library Base: 28615
20-inch Poppy Cone: 1531
   Twisted Vine base: 443
16-inch Poinsettia: 1557
   Small Lion's Paw base: 481
18-inch Grapevine: 348
   Large Tree Trunk base: 342
18-inch Trumpet Vine: 346
   Large Tree Trunk base: 342
18-inch Wisteria Vine: 342
   Large Tree Trunk base: 342
20-inch Poppy Cone: 1531
   Blown-glass Crab base: 398
18-inch Tulip Dome: 1596
   Library base: 363
22-inch Nasturtium Turban: 1506
   Root base: 393

22-inch Laburnum: 1539
   Bird Skeleton base: 442
18-inch Cobweb and Apple
      Blossom: 151
   Wheat Mosaic base: 151
20-inch Azalea Turban: 1918
   Root Ball base: 390
22-inch Tulip: 1546
   Large Library base: 367
18-inch Peacock: 1472
   Peacock base: 1455
24-inch Border Peony: 1574
   Senior floor base: 379
28-inch Peony Bouquet Cone: 603
14-inch Dragonfly: 1585
   Dragonfly Mosaic base: 356
20-inch Dragonfly: 1495
   Original Tiffany base: 8619
18-inch Peony Turban: 1475
   Library base: 546
22-inch Elaborate Peony Turban: 1903
   Large Lion's Paw base: 391

20-inch Azalea Turban on a Root Ball base, with details

22-inch Tulip on a Large Library base, with details

24-inch Border Peony on a Senior Floor base, with details

28-inch Peony Bouquet Cone with details

14-inch Dragonfly on a Dragonfly Mosaic base

22-inch Elaborate Peony Turban on
a Large Lion's Paw base, with details

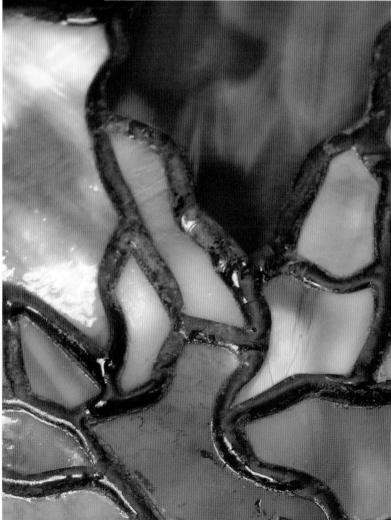

20-inch Dragonfly on an original Tiffany base, with details

The distinctive patina on this original Tiffany base offers an excellent illustration of what the lamp artist should strive to duplicate.

18-inch Peony Turban on a Library base

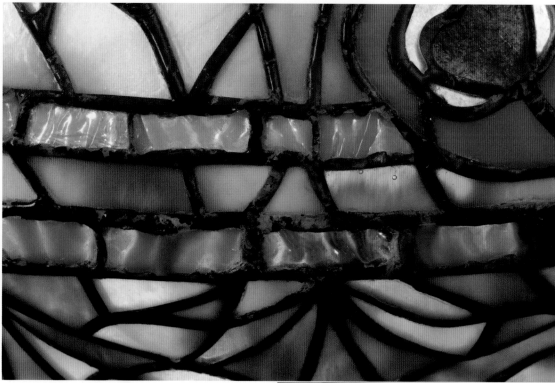

18-inch Peacock on a Peacock base, with details

More details from the 18-inch Peacock